GET
THAT
JOB

Tools, Techniques, and Strategies "Borrowed" From Successful Job Applicants

BY RUBY N. GORTER

Copyright © 1997 by

)KS
venue
ork 11944

erved

Library of Congress Catalog Card Number: 97-9224

Library of Congress Cataloging in Publication Data

Gorter, Ruby N.
how to ... Get That Job!: tools, techniques & strategies "borrowed" from successful job applicants / by Ruby N. Gorter.
     p.cm. — (the *how to do it* series)
  ISBN 0-87576-201-8 (pbk.)
1. Applications for positions. 2. Employment interviewing.
3. Vocational guidance. I. Title II.
Series: *how to do it* series. (Greenport, N. Y.)
HF5383.g58 1997
650. 14--dc21   97-9224

                               CIP

Printed in the United States of America

ABOUT THE AUTHOR

During her twenty years in human resources, Ruby Gorter interviewed and placed hundreds of successful job applicants. But it bothered her to see how many qualified people were turned away simply because they did not understand how to present themselves at an interview.

She accumulated material on the secret tips, methods and techniques that make some job applicants so successful and compiled this data into "how to GET THAT JOB." Ms. Gorter has also written for various publications including a bi-weekly column for a Michigan newspaper. She is now the owner of a successful secretarial business and conducts seminars preparing high school students for today's challenging job market.

Ms. Gorter lives in Oregon with her husband, Jack. They have two married sons and are the proud grandparents of five wonderful grandchildren.

"Successful applicants really do have techniques and secrets that put them ahead of others" says Ms. Gorter, "Well, they're not secrets any more. It's my intention to give everybody an equal opportunity to be hired for a job that's right for them".

TABLE OF CONTENTS

PREFACE

Remember when you were first learning to ride a bicycle? Balancing was almost impossible, especially since you were always afraid of falling over. But, with practice, you were soon racing against the wind and biking was almost as easy as walking.

Learning the techniques of successful job applicants is not so different from learning how to ride a bike. You must first discover the techniques of how to do it properly, then practice them. Soon you'll enjoy the results...in this case, getting the job that's right for you.

"**how to GET THAT JOB**" cannot guarantee a job, but the tips, techniques and exercises in this book will show you exactly how to develop an organized and productive job search. I recommend that you read the entire book first, then go back to the beginning and complete each exercise.

Good luck...you're on your way!

CHAPTER 1

WHERE DO I START?

Start with yourself. Just for fun, imagine you're a new gadget. Your inventors want everybody to buy you. You, of course, can't help because you don't know what your benefits are, you're only a gadget. But your inventors know how good you are, so they tell potential buyers all about your benefits, your value and your accomplishments. Before you know it, you're part of the consumer's life.

It's exactly the same for a job applicant...except you get to be both the inventor and the gadget. Just as the inventors gave consumers reasons to buy the gadget, you have to present your benefits, value and accomplishments to potential employers and give them reasons to hire you.

Like I said, start with yourself:

    1) Establish what's important to you.
    2) Find the job you will enjoy most.
    3) Discover and Define your accomplishments.

1. Establish what's important to you.

Many of us choose jobs based solely on money, prestige or social status and that's too bad. Your position contributes enormously to your sense of self-worth and enjoyment of life. If you're not happy doing a job, you'll probably be out looking for another one within a short time.

So, how do you know which job is the one for you? The answer is **evaluate what's important to you.**

A job based on what's important to you is the right one for you!

I have a friend who was considered very successful, by me and just about everyone who knew her. She worked for a prestigious firm, earned a lot of money but rarely looked forward to going to work or had a smile on her face. It was my impression she was unhappy with her company but, to my surprise, it wasn't *where* she worked but *what she was doing*. She needed to find what was important to her and do it.

No, she didn't quit her job. What she did was change from full to part-time work and, in her spare time, she now paints and sells her watercolors at bazaars and flea markets. That's what's important to her and what was missing from her earlier job situation. She's a far happier person today and it's no longer necessary for me to turn her upside-down to see a smile on her face.

> **SECRET: By establishing what's important to you, you'll be saving valuable time by targeting your job search to the kind of job you'll enjoy.**

The following exercise contains questions to help you determine what's important to you in a job. Circle "Yes" or "No" for each question and **don't think too much before circling! The first answer that pops into your head is probably the right one, even if it surprises you!**

How important are people to you? Do you . . .

Prefer working alone?	Yes	No
Work best with less than three other people?	Yes	No

Appreciate the hustle and bustle of many co-workers? Yes No
Like meeting new people each day? Yes No
Enjoy working with children? Yes No
Prefer being around older people? Yes No
Feel more comfortable among the young? Yes No
Enjoy helping others? Yes No
Find something "good" in everyone , even when the Wicked
Witch of the North comes to call? Yes No
Take a long time before trusting and making friends? Yes No

What else is important to you? Do you...

Enjoy being around animals more than people? Yes No
Have a million plants and they're all thriving? Yes No
Love working with your hands and can fix just about
anything? Yes No

Are you a person who . . .

Prefers assignments that are mentally demanding? Yes No
Find yourself doing sports that have a certain amount of risk-
taking? (If yes, you are the type that needs challenges and a
little risk in your life such as airline steward, ambulance
driver, fire-fighter, police work.) Yes No
Needs to know friends and relatives respect the job you do?
Yes No
Is always organized and on time? Yes No
Likes to stay up and get up late? Yes No
Is and always has been an early bird? Yes No
Has a gift of gab and could sell anyone the Brooklyn Bridge?
Yes No

What about personal freedom? Are you someone who . . .

Would like to work in the great outdoors?	Yes	No
Likes the idea of a job that requires traveling?	Yes	No
Hates to work weekends or long hours?	Yes	No
Performs better under flexible working hours?	Yes	No
Is happy with an established work schedule?	Yes	No

Must have windows in your work environment or you feel trapped? Yes No

How important is the money you earn?

Is financial security a must? Yes No

Are rapid advancements and increased earnings of great importance? Yes No

Is working your way up financially in an organization a challenge? Yes No

Is variety important? Do you . . .

Prefer working at a fast pace ? Yes No

Like to take on new tasks? Yes No

Feel good when you're given responsibilities that challenge your abilities? Yes No

Enjoy the idea of moving to different locations with job advancements? Yes No

Constantly listen to music and/or play an instrument? Yes No
(If yes, you are the type of person that works best with busy activity around you)

Works best with busy activity around you? Yes No

Enjoy the challenge of meeting sudden deadlines? Yes No

Prefer a rapidly growing organization that frequently adds new people and tasks? Yes No

Thrives on competition from fellow employees?   Yes   No
Appreciates a job with a certain amount of risk-taking?   Yes   No

*What importance does a peaceful job environment have to
you? Do you ...*

Accomplish more when alone or with only a few others
around you?   Yes   No
(If yes, you require little or no supervision and are a self starter)
Enjoy doing crossword puzzles and word searches?   Yes   No
(If yes, you are the type of person who works best in a quiet
environment)
Appreciate a small office atmosphere?   Yes   No
Feel satisfied just doing a job well?   Yes   No
Prefer tasks that require precision and exactness?   Yes   No
Favor a job with a predictable work routine?   Yes   No
Enjoy a job that has repetitive tasks?   Yes   No
Need a patient, soft spoken employer?   Yes   No

Is authority an important issue? Do you ...

Like to be in charge of others?   Yes   No
Work best when under another's direction?   Yes   No
Feel uncomfortable taking direction from others?   Yes   No
Tend to be defiant to anyone "telling you what to do?   Yes   No
Requires little or no guidance from others, a self-starter?
    Yes   No
Wants to be an expert in your field?   Yes   No

Are you creative? Are you the person who

Can make a delicious meal out of anything?   Yes   No
Fixes friends' makeup so they look prettier?   Yes   No

9

Always cuts and arranges your family's hair?	Yes	No
Everybody turns to when they want to change their living room?	Yes	No
Can smell a fine antique a mile away?	Yes	No
Writes in their spare time and sends letters that people keep and read aloud?	Yes	No
Doodles, draws caricatures and cartoons everybody loves?	Yes	No
Can make a drab outfit look fabulous with touches only you can create?	Yes	No
Designs and sews your own clothing?	Yes	No

Now that you've finished, use a brightly colored hi-lighter and highlight your "yes" answers. This will be the guide you'll use to help you decide what kind of job is best for you. Circle your "Nos" with a different colored hi-lighter to remind you about what you don't want in a job.

2. Find the job you'll enjoy most.

Wouldn't it be great if you discovered a job where all of your "yesses" were included? That's about as likely as eating anything you want and not worrying about the scale screaming "overload". Realistically, just as we have to watch our calories, we have to watch for the job opportunity that has more of our "yesses" than "no's". Find that job and you will probably be more than satisfied doing it.

Quick story: Once upon a time there was a high school girl who wanted to become a fashion designer. She was always in her bedroom drawing pictures of exotic clothing and dreaming of a glamorous working studio filled with expensive art and furniture. One day her mother came into her room and reprimanded her: "Maria, just look at your window. Why, it's so dirty, I can't see the beautiful flower garden below." "Mom," replied Maria calmly, "if I wanted to see out the window, I'd just raise it!"

Well, Maria did go on to become a successful fashion designer and did work in a lavish studio filled with expensive furniture and art. But if anyone wanted to see out the windows, they'd still have to raise them. I would say she definitely had a "No" under "must have windows in the work environment."

Now that you've pinpointed what's important to you, let's start listing job opportunities that include these elements. For example, if you marked "Yes" for "enjoy being around animals more than people", list vet assistant, a receptionist at a vet's or groomer's, clerk at a pet shop, or a salesperson selling pet supplies, dog or horse trainer, or assistant to either. If you also answered "Yes" to design and sew your own clothing, how about designing clothing and accessories for animals? See how easy it is?

If you marked "Yes" for "prefer working in the great outdoors", think of jobs like working in a nursery, selling real estate, traveling salesperson (especially if you marked "Yes" for loves to travel too), auto sales, park ranger, toll booth operator, landscape designer, construction worker, athletic director, assistant to sports director (schools, nursing homes, etc.). Enjoy working in the great outdoors and love to travel? Consider an activities director on a cruise liner!

If you marked "Yes" to "sell anyone the Brooklyn Bridge", telemarketing is a great job opportunity! Did you answer "Yes" to "can make a drab outfit look fabulous"? How about a salesperson at a womans' clothing store, fashion designer or designer coordinator? Enjoy working with children? Child photographer's assistant, owner of children's clothing store and school aid come to mind.

If you're somebody who wants a secure '9 - 5-er' as a word processor, secretary, administrative assistant or receptionist but still have some exciting "yesses" marked, then do the job you're comfortable with...in an exciting place. How about a receptionist at a modeling agency or secretary to the editor of a glamorous magazine? Like to help people? Focus on charitable organizations, hospitals and other places where your desire to help others can be a real plus.

"Yes" to "constantly listens to music":, "like meeting new people" and "happier with routine work schedule"? Why not a clerk at a record shop? The secret to finding the job that is best for you is to target jobs that include as many of your "Yesses" as you can! And this is a good time to point out that almost any job can be a stepping stone to bigger and better things...if you want it to be. Set your sights on your eventual career goal and choose the job that'll get you there with time, patience and hard work.

When you think you've covered all your job possibilities do this:

• Ask friends and relatives what careers they think might be appropriate for you (their answers may surprise you) and add them to your list.

• Visit your local library and go through The Dictionary of Occupational Titles (DOT). Take a pen and plenty of paper with you. This dictionary appears to have a never ending list of occupations and you should discover many career opportunities.

Once you begin your search, you'll be surprised how fast your list grows and how many career choices you have. Now comes the "big decision"...which one? Make **three career choices** from your list. It'll be easier to make them if you review your "Yes" list. The three that contain the most "Yesses" are the ones to choose.

You may be wondering why you should pick three possible careers instead of one. Another quick story: When I entered junior high, I decided nursing was my vocation. The physical and mental demands, the concept of helping others, and the fact that this career would earn the respect of my friends and relatives were all appealing. My mother was very wise. When she learned I was planning to attend nursing classes after graduation, she suggested I volunteer as a candy striper at the local hospital where I could get first-hand experience watching nurses in action. I soon discovered that nursing involved more than crisp, white uniforms and dispensing medicine and advice to patients. I watched the nurses clean up after patients who couldn't keep their meals down and change dressings that were definitely unappetizing. I watched and then I threw up. So much for that career.

I was lucky. Before I wasted my time and money training for a career that was inappropriate, I discovered I couldn't handle the "down side" of nursing. You, too, may discover unappealing aspects to one or two of your choices. Research first, then make your decision about the career you're considering. Here's how:

Use your library

Locate and read reference material about the career choices or kinds of corporations that appeal to you. Autobiographies, if appropriate, will provide important insights. If you already know you want to work in an office, research different kinds of companies and select those which are attractive to you. If you're interested in language, for example, choose a multinational company. Some office workers are drawn to legal work, advertising agencies or the fashion industry. There's a wide variety of choices in office careers.

Utilize Temporary Services

Temporary employment agencies are another resource for choosing a career. Temporary work gives you the chance to explore work environments and an excellent way to discover more about how well you and your career match up. Besides the usual secretarial and selling jobs, many manufacturing companies utilize temp agencies to choose employees who will be offered a permanent position in their factory. If you're career "picks' include a job in which you enjoy repetition, precision and predictability, factory work just might be for you. What better way to discover if that's true?

Ask Questions

Ask friends, relatives and associates about their jobs, if you think you might like what they do. Find out as much as you can. The two questions that will give you the most insights are: what do they like best and least about the job. Then ask questions about what's important to you. Does this career involve long hours and weekend responsibilities? Is there a certain amount of risk-taking? How frequently can one be promoted? The more questions you ask, the more you'll know about the job you're researching.

Don't panic if you don't know anyone to ask. In that case, try approaching a company that would employ someone with your career goals and ask for a 10-minute interview with a person in your field. People love answering questions about themselves (don't you?) and, by doing so, you'll learn the pros and cons of a job, and that could be the deciding factor in your final career choice.

Now take a deep breath: it's time to make "the big decision. From your three job possibilities, you must select the one that's best for you. Just for fun, look at the problem this way: pretend you're secretly married to all three jobs. Since being a bigamist is illegal you must divorce two of your mates. You like them all but which one do you keep?

Begin by drawing one wide and three skinny (to the right) columns down a sheet of note paper. Head the skinny columns with your three job possibilities. Under the wide column, list each question you answered 'yes" to in the previous questionnaire. Then, next to the question, put a giant "X" under each job that has that "yes" to offer. You will quickly see which of the jobs has the most "yesses". If it's a close-call, add up the "yesses" to find out which is the "winner" for you.

Congratulations, you have now divorced the two less desirable "mates" and selected the one (job) that will give you the greatest satisfaction in your working life

Now that you know which job will make you happiest, set your sights on it, complete any training (if necessary) and then prepare to GET THAT JOB! Again, don't discount the importance of temporarily taking a "stepping stone" job in order to work your way up through the ranks. Stepping stones are frequently used to reach the other side of the river.

If your chosen career does require special training or additional education, here's what to do:

- Check the yellow pages of your telephone directory under your career choice for trade schools.
- Write to National Association of Trade and Technical Schools, 2251 Wisconsin Ave., NW, Washington, DC 2007 for a directory of trade and technical schools.
- Investigate local schools, universities, and colleges for co-op work study programs or internship programs in your chosen field.
- Write Cooperative Education Assoc., 655 15th Street, NW, Washington, D.C. 2007 for a list of schools offering co-op programs.
- Look into home study programs. For information, write National Home Study Council, 1601 18th Street, NW, Washington, DC 20009.

3. Discover and Define your accomplishments.

A word of caution: you're probably eager to begin your job search and may be thinking of skipping or skimming these pages. Please don't. Take the time to read this book thoroughly and do the exercises carefully... "how to GET THAT JOB!" was created to give you the information, techniques and procedures that successful applicants use in their own job campaigns. You'll have plenty of time to actively begin your job search *after you are fully equipped with the right tools.*

Now you're ready to discover and define your accomplishments. Don't have any you say? Not true. We accomplish something every day of our lives, we just have to know how to identify them. So, even if this is your first time seeking employment or you're back in the job market after a time away, relax.

16

Chances are you'll revise your thinking about your accomplishments after you read the examples and complete the exercises on the next few pages.

Here's the first example to give you a general idea of what I'm talking about:

A senior high school cheerleader was applying for a part-time clerical position. She astonished the interviewer by saying she had never accomplished anything. This was her first attempt at getting a job she explained and, until she did, how could she list any work accomplishments? If this cheerleader had known how to recognize her accomplishments, she would have looked at her situation like this:

I'm the head cheerleader with responsibility for getting the other cheerleaders together for practice, bringing in new cheers, keeping the crowd involved and letting the team players know they're supported. What are my accomplishments in terms of getting a job? I . . .

1) Manage my "staff", the other cheerleaders.
2) Motivate a large gathering of people.
3) Deliver a service (creating enthusiasm).
4) Establish routines.
5) Encourage the team players.
6) Develop new motivating tools.

I'd hire her, wouldn't you?

Here's another example, which you may recognize.

17

When Mrs. Unknown's last child left the nest, she enjoyed the freedom of doing whatever she pleased. Briefly. Then she became restless and realized she wanted a career. Although she felt confident in her job choice, Mrs. Unknown felt immense anxiety about competing against a multitude of other applicants with recent job experience. What could she offer compared to them?

Plenty. For the record, I have never believed in the term "just a housewife". Whenever these words rolled apologetically off the lips of the many women I've interviewed, I always cringed. I genuinely believe housewives have more accomplishments to boast about than almost any other career. If they took the time to list them, it would be impossible to fit them all into a one page resume.

Now, if Mrs. Unknown had read this book, she would have discovered that during those years of being a housewife and mom, she . . .

1) Created a nurturing environment.
2) Researched, acquired and prepared nourishing, well balanced meals.
3) Administered appropriate medication.
4) Designed and managed a utilitarian, attractive home setting.
5) Provided a role model and good example to members of her family.

Quite an accomplished woman, I'd say. Could she be you?

Be creative, use your imagination and discover your accomplishments! Here's how you do it:

First, on a separate sheet of paper, list each position you 've ever held (housewife, student, etc., are jobs too!). Then make a list of every activity for which you were responsible. We'll call this the "Yawn" description" (A) of your job. Leave two generous spaces after each responsibility so you can add (B) and (C).

Next, using the "Word Bank" page 21, transform your "Yawn" description" to one that "Sizzles" and write that under the other. (You'll find out how in a moment).

Three, under each new "Sizzle" description, describe what you had to do to complete the tasks assigned to you, in other words, define your accomplishments (D).

To help you get started, here's an example: You are a clerk at a grocery store, and you want to apply for a good job and send in a super fantastic resume, but - you say - you're just a clerk at a grocery store. **What do you mean, just a grocery clerk?!!** Let me show you how important you are and what you have accomplished!

List all your responsibilities. Let's start with:

(A) Set up aisle displays. (yawn)

Obviously, we need to embellish on this and transform this responsibility with words that "sizzle" (B) from the Sizzle List.

(A) Set up aisle displays.

(B) Designed, created and improved aisle display designs. (sizzle)

Now we need to describe what you did in order to design, create and improve the aisle displays, in other words, **define your accomplishment!** (C)

(A) Set up isle displays. (yawn)

(B) Designed, created and improved isle display designs. (sizzle)

(C) I created a system that prominently displayed new, attractive packaging at customer eye level, clearly marked sale items and made older, less appealing packaging accessible but less conspicuous. (accomplishment)

Here are a few more responsibilities I've transformed using the same procedure... just to demonstrate how easy it is to do...and what difference it makes to how your duties will appear to a potential employer.

(A) Helped customers. (yawn)

(B) Politely assisted and guided customers. (sizzle)

(C) I thoroughly familiarized myself with the store floor plan so I was able to quickly and accurately direct customers to the products they were seeking. (accomplishments)

(A) Swept assigned areas. (yawn)

(B) Inspected, monitored and improved the appearance of assigned areas. (sizzle)

(C) I developed a vigilant routine that maintained my assigned area in a way that was attractive, neat and clean at all times. (accomplishment)

And you thought because you were **just a clerk,** you had no accomplishments?

4. "Sizzle Word Bank"

The "Word Bank" consists of action words that add "sizzle" to your responsibilities. Many words could be added to this list, and each time you think of one, be sure and write it down with the others.

"Sizzle" Word Bank

Accelerated	Formulated	Presented
Accomplished	Founded	Processed
Achieved	Fulfilled	Procured
Administered	Gathered	Programmed
Allocated	Generated	Promoted
Assisted	Guided	Recommended
Balanced	Increased	Reconciled
Charted	Illustrated	Recorded
Classified	Implemented	Recruited
Communicated	Improved	Reduced
Completed	Increased	Referred
Composed	Influenced	Reorganized
Constructed	Initiated	Reported
Consulted	Inspected	Researched
Coordinated	Instructed	Resolved
Counseled	Interviewed	Restored
Created	Issued	Reviewed
Decreased	Launched	Sanctioned
Demonstrated	Located	Scheduled
Designed	Maintained	Secured
Developed	Monitored	Stabilized
Directed	Motivated	Supervised
Displayed	Negotiated	Supplemented
Established	Observed	Supported
Estimated	Obtained	Trained
Evaluated	Organized	Taught
Exhibited	Participated	Updated
Expanded	Performed	Upgraded
Expedited	Planned	Won
Facilitated	Prepared	Wrote

Finished with the exercise? Good. Now take a look at all you've accomplished. Doesn't it make you feel more confident? It should if you did it properly. Be sure and keep this paper to guide you when writing your cover letters and resumes and to remind you of all you've accomplished.

Next - and this may sound silly but is very important - stand in front of a mirror and rehearse, out loud, reciting each accomplishment again and again until they are firmly implanted in your memory. You'll be amazed at how quickly you remember them. The reason, of course, is you're remembering what you accomplished. This will also build your confidence and you'll **bring that confidence with you to the job search experience.**

SECRET: Successful applicants discover their accomplishments and develop them into tools that get jobs.

CHAPTER 2

HOW DO I PREPARE
FOR A SUCCESSFUL JOB CAMPAIGN?

Your mental attitude is vital to getting the job that's important to you. How you feel about yourself is relayed to others so.....

Develop a positive attitude.

" I'm too old," "I'm too young," "I don't have enough experience," are just excuses. Furthermore, they drastically reduce your chances for employment. Believe it, no one is going to hire you just to make you feel better about yourself! When you feel good about yourself, others feel good about you too.

Avoid negative remarks about your search.

Don't let anybody tell you how difficult it is to get into the field you've chosen or that the economy is so bad getting a job is impossible. Do what you can to avoid - or ignore - those who deliver such messages and keep a positive attitude.

Make job hunting a full-time job.

Many applicants race to the newsstand each day, circle the classifieds that interest them, send out their resumes then sit and wait for a reply. This is called a "part-time job." To achieve the results you want, use every available moment for your job search, just as if you were being paid to find that opening.

> **SECRET: Successful applicants realize a job search campaign is a full-time job!**

Start each morning as if you were going to work.

It's all too easy to fall into the habit of getting up when you feel like, neglecting personal hygiene and getting appropriately dressed only when you need to BUT these habits encourage depression, destroy self-motivation and can lower self-esteem. So set the alarm each night and get out of bed when it goes off. Shower, dress and get yourself looking like you would if you were going to work. Then go to work...at finding that job. You'll soon be dressing for work because you *are* going to work.

Create an office-like atmosphere within your home.

Job opportunities have been lost because of misplaced information so it's vitally important to organize properly. Designate a work area for yourself. If you have a desk, great, if not it's no problem. Some applicants use the kitchen counter or dining room table and keep certain drawers specifically for work notes or contact names. Place the telephone nearby, along with your research material and important contact information, and make all calls from there. You'll find that by doing this, you're feel more alert and professional when making telephone contacts and you'll sound that way to the people you're calling.

Organize your job search.

Many of us have trouble remembering names and telephone numbers and it's even harder when you're bombarded with a lot of contact names and related job information. That's why it's essential to create a well-organized system for keeping your collected job information and contacts. Whatever method you use, make sure your system includes a way to update your files as your job search continues.

Allocate enough time for research

Ever wonder why a position was offered to another applicant even though you were more experienced and qualified? Perhaps that applicant took the time to learn about the company and knew how to utilize that information to win the job. Employers are more impressed with resumes, letters and interviews that reflect research done by the applicant, basically because research reflects *interest*, *motivation* and *initiative*.

> **SECRET: Successful applicants research and use the information they gather as tools to generate employer interest.**

Schedule your job search activities.

Once you've accepted the fact that your career search is a full-time job, you need to allocate how much time you'll devote to different areas of the search. Too much in one area means too little time in another. At the beginning of each week do this:

• Break down the research you'll be doing and allocate the time needed to complete everything in a reasonable amount of time.

• Figure out how much time you should spend making telephone calls to find contacts, following up leads, answering ads, networking, setting up appointments and calling to set up job research interviews.

• Establish the amount of time you should spend preparing and typing cover letters, resumes and thank you notes.

• Estimate how much time you'll need to cover job research interviews.

• Plan on a minimum of three to four hours a week for job interviews.

You can't always expect to adhere to a strict time limit for each task but knowing you only have an hour to finish typing cover letters or a few minutes to finish those calls, will motivate you to get the job done and faster than you would without specific scheduling guidelines. But don't be too hard on yourself. Allow yourself some time after "work"- for fun and relaxation. A relaxed job candidate is a successful one.

Establish goals.

Ask any successful job applicant and they'll tell you: **goals are essential in an effective job search.** Sticking to their own personal accomplishment goals helps them stay on the right track and get that job ahead of the others. The successful applicant:

• Makes as many calls as needed each day to obtain a minimum of five job research interviews (job research interviews are described in Chapter 4)

- Arranges at least five job research interviews and, from them, a minimum of two referrals.

- Researches no less than sixty companies where they might want to work. (I know it sounds like a lot of work but it's worth it. Chapter 3 will show you how to locate these companies and what to do when you have.)

- Develops a follow-up plan for all leads, contacts and referrals.

SECRET: The successful applicant sets weekly goals and sticks to them.

CHAPTER 3

WHERE DO I FIND COMPANIES THAT WOULD HIRE ME?

Concentrate on targeting companies that hire applicants with your career goals. Your objective is to locate and research a minimum of sixty organizations that interest you, even though a position has not been advertised. *Successful applicants know that 80% to 90% of all job opportunities are never advertised!* So, get busy and compile that list of 60 target companies, you won't regret it.

Finding your target companies.

1. YELLOW PAGES

For those of you who have chosen a career such as a legal secretary, you will probably find all 60 of the organizations you need to research in a matter of minutes (you'd simply look under Lawyers). But what if you selected a career that is not so obvious and under a single heading? *Check for hidden opportunities in all headings!*

Say your ideal position would be in a travel agency. You check the heading in the yellow pages under travel agencies and find only fifteen. Okay. What about the headings : "Railroad Ticket Agencies;" "Aircraft Charter & Rental"; "Airline Companies"; and "Passport & Visa Services?" Or, you love to work with your hands and are artistic so you decided arranging flowers would be perfect for you. Look under "Florists" and "Flower

28

Arranging", of course. But also: "Plants, Interior Design & Maintenance;" "Plant Shops"; and "Plants, Living-Renting & Leasing." Then go further afield. Some "Nurseries" offer plants and landscape designing, ideal if outside work was important to you!

Scan the index section of the yellow pages and look for hidden opportunities!

2. NETWORKING

Don't keep your job search hidden. Talk about it with friends, relatives, business associates and contacts. The more people know, the better the chance that someone will remember a company that has an opening, where your talents might be of use or can provide you with a referral. Successful applicants use people they know to get remarkable results. But you have to know **how** to get their help or you'll have little success accessing this precious resource.

Lean a little

My definition of "leaning" is relying upon people for advice and encouragement. Don't confuse it with begging which is asking for charity and definitely not advisable. Your friends may enjoy helping and advising you but when asked to "find" you a job, relations become strained...at best. So, don't beg! Or you'll discover the adult version of hide and seek...and you'll be doing the seeking.

Treat your friends & relatives as business associates
first and friends second.

Here's an example of why this is so important: Jim, unemployed, called his friend Bob who worked at a firm that was a potential employer for Jim. He asked for and received a job research interview at Bob's office. Jim arrived for the appointment half an hour late and, because he and Bob were friends, thought it unnecessary to apologize or explain. He hadn't taken the time to dress professionally but presented himself in blue jeans and a sport shirt. The actual interview also left a lasting impression on Bob.

Jim: "I'm supposed to ask you these questions. Read them over and I'll write down the answers. Hell, I forgot my pen. Got one? Thanks. Hey, I got something to do, why don't you read over the questions, write in the answers and I'll pick them up later, okay?"

If you were in Bob's place, would you feel comfortable referring Jim to one of your professional contacts or offering him a position in your firm? Unlikely. Now Jim would never treat business contacts in such a manner, but, because Bob was a friend, he saw no reason to treat the interview professionally.

If, on the other hand, Jim had approached the interview as if he were meeting with a stranger, things would have been different. Of course he would be on time, dressed appropriately and prepared with pen and paper.

Jim: Bob, thanks for seeing me today. I know how busy you are so I'll stick to my ten minutes, as promised. Ready to begin? Fine. Let me ask you ....."

Jim has now demonstrated a sincere desire to learn about his chosen career, presented himself in a professional manner and acknowledged his friend as an important resource. Would Bob now feel comfortable helping Jim in his job search? What do you think?

3. CLASSIFIED ADS

There are opportunities in the classified ads and I'm not suggesting you ignore them. But you should realize that, for every resume you send in response to an ad, there are a multitude of others doing the same thing. In most cases, the name of the company is not listed or the identity of the person hiring revealed. Ideally, you should know the company, its background, and to whom your resume should be directed when applying for a position. The reasons will be discussed in later chapters.

If you're already working, an embarrassing possibility is that you might send your resume to a post office box number, only to discover that it's the organization where you are already employed!

4. EMPLOYMENT AGENCIES

While it's true that employment agencies have openings that may not appear in the classified section, professional agencies have to screen applicants **based on the employers' preconceived idea of the perfect candidate's qualifications.** So if a potential employer, for example, specifies someone with sales experience, even though you have accomplishments that make such a placement appropriate, you'd be "screened out" immediately. Whereby if you had the chance to write and/or speak directly with the decision maker, you'd have the opportunity to make your value and accomplishments known. **Employers' hiring decisions are not necessarily based only on degrees and experience.**

If you did your homework and fell short of the 60 targeted companies, don't worry. Use what you have (remembering that more **is** better) and begin the next step...research.

Find out all you can about your targeted companies: how long they've been in business, how many people they employ, what they make or the service they offer, etc. You can find the answers to many questions in books such as Standard and Poor's, Moody's and Dun & Bradstreet, all at your local library. Don't be surprised if some of your targeted companies are not listed. They may be relatively new or too small to be in these reference books. Set them aside and, later, visit or call them and ask for informational brochures. Your local chamber of commerce is another place to find corporate literature. In addition, new companies in town are often introduced through material found at the chamber of commerce.

CHAPTER 4

THE ALL IMPORTANT JOB RESEARCH INTERVIEW

Job research interviews are undoubtedly one of the most valuable parts of your job-seeking campaign. They are how you gather **specific job-related information** and are designed to give you:

1) Salary ranges (very important at job interviews!)
2) Criteria (hiring standards for the job, see Criteria, later in this chapter)
3) **Referrals, referrals, referrals!**

Convinced they're important? Good. Let's begin.

Select your targets

Your previous research resulted in an impressive list of potential employers. You're now ready to select fifty companies to target as job possibilities. List each on a 3 x 5 index card, making sure you've included all pertinent information. If you have difficulty deciding which to select, choose those companies where you would most like to work (right size, type of industry etc.) After you have made your choices, put the list away for future use and file the targeted companies in a 3 x 5 card file, ready to use.

Find the right contact

You'll need to find the name, correct spelling and title of the person responsible for hiring within your job area at each company you want to contact. That's a lot of calls so you might want to asks friends or family members to help you. Be specific when asking who hires in your field. The person who hires the secretarial pool is probably not the same as the one who hires the sales staff. For goodness sakes, don't be afraid to make these calls. The worst that could happen is:

- The person on the other end won't understand what you're talking about.
- You'll be told there are no job openings, even though you didn't ask that.
- The telephone line will suddenly go dead which is annoying, but nothing more.

Remember, if you're unsuccessful, you can always call back at a later date or have your helper do it. **You need those names and titles.**

SECRET: You may be the best qualified person but, when you hear about an opening and contact the wrong person, one with little or no hiring authority, you may have lost your chance at the job.

A sample call:

You: Good morning. I need the name of the person who hires your sales staff. Could you tell me who that is, please?
Voice: We have no openings in sales right now.
You: I understand that, I only want to send some information.
Voice: Oh, his name is James Green.
You: Is that spelled G R E E N?
Voice: That's right.
You: Thank you and may I have his title?
Voice: Personnel director.
You: Great. Thanks a lot for your help.

It's not uncommon for vendors and potential customers to call companies for similar information so you'll find most businesses are more than willing to give you names and titles. If you discover a company is no longer in business or has relocated, be sure to replace it with another company from your original list of targets.

Select Five

Now you have the right contacts for each of your targeted companies. Select five for your job research interviews **but don't use the companies where you'd most like to work.**

Setting Up Job Research Interviews

Ready? It's time to start calling and setting up job research interviews. Some applicants feel uneasy about these "cold calls" but - please - don't worry, others call without preparation too. Besides, you have an advantage, you're armed with information about the company you're calling and you know the name of the person who hires in your job area.

Now, let's make that first call!

You: Good morning. May I please speak to Mr. James?
Voice: May I tell him who's calling?
You: My name is Marcy Williams.
Voice: May I tell him what this is in regard to?
You: Yes, I'm in the process of researching hiring standards in the secretarial field, and Mr. James could be a valuable resource for me. May I please speak with him about possibly setting up an interview?

Voice: One moment please.

Mr. James: Hello, this is Mr. James.

You: Mr. James, thank you for taking my call. I'm researching the standards by which secretaries are hired, and hoped you would be willing to help. It will take only 10 minutes of your time. Could we set up an appointment?

Mr. James: I guess I can talk to you for a few minutes. How about Monday .....

Don't give up if the first few calls result in negative responses. Keep trying and, with practice and experience, you're sure to succeed. Your goal is to obtain five job research interviews.

THE TEN MINUTE JOB RESEARCH INTERVIEW

One of the most important reasons for this interview is to establish the criteria, or hiring standards, for the job you're pursuing. Let's talk about criteria for a moment, they're important.

Untrained applicants often don't know the criteria for the job they're seeking, a potentially costly mistake. Remember, there are usually many applicants applying for the same position and potential employers look for resumes, cover letters and interviews that show the applicant **knows and meets the criteria essential to the job.**

Let's say somebody wants a job in customer service and asked three different people in the field what they would look for in a candidate. The finished list would probably look like this:

Customer Service Criteria:

1) Communicates well, both verbaly and in writing.
2) Plans and organizes effectively.
3) Knows how to listen.
4) Sets and achieves goals.
5) Demonstrate personal computer skills.
6) Anticipates the needs of a client.
7) Enjoys meeting new people.
8) Works well under pressure.

This applicant now knows the standards by which he or she would be measured and has acquired one of the many "tools" successful applicants utilize in cover letters, resumes and job interviews .

Back to the job research interview. Here's a good way to start:

You: Thank you for taking the time to meet with me, Mr/Mrs...... I know you're busy so I'll be brief. As I mentioned on the phone, I'm interested in **learning about what you look for in a candidate for a secretarial position with your firm.**

If your contact hesitates before answering, give an example to clarify (and impress with your knowledge) such as:

You: "I know the applicant would need both verbal and written skills but what other qualities would you say are essential to the job?"

Write down the answer. Don't talk while writing (silence

indicates how serious you are about getting *all* the information correctly). After you're finished repeat it back: "You said one should be able to learn quickly, thank you. Next?"

Repeat this procedure after *each new employment qualification.* The purpose of restating is to convey the importance of the information to you and show that you are really serious about recording it correctly. *Successful applicants know the importance of this strategy and use it.*

If you don't understand some answers, *don't interrupt.* Put a check mark by any answers that require clarification. When your contact cannot add anything further, show your gratitude for the information given.

"That's a big help. You've told me a lot I didn't know. Let me quickly go over what you said so I know I haven't missed anything . . . "

Then repeat each topic on your list. Again, *successful applicants understand the importance of this repetition.* Your contact can now make corrections and possibly add more points. You also made him or her feel important and useful. When you ask for referrals later, you'll probably get them.

Once the list is complete, clarify those you checked earlier. You: "You mentioned being familiar with MS-DOS was important. Does that mean programming is part of the job requirement?"

Once you've completed the criteria, it's time to ask the following questions:

1) In your opinion, would you say the turnover rate for secretaries here is high or relatively low?
2) What are the salary ranges for this job? (Be sure you get the full range, from beginner to most experienced).
3) Are there promotions in this field, and if so, what would be the next level?

By this time, you'll probably feel comfortable enough to tackle the other important reason for the interview: **Asking for a job research referral.**

You: "I'm really grateful for the time you spent with me, thank you very much. By the way, Mr. Smith, can you think of someone I might contact who could also help me learn more about the career I'm pursuing? Anyone you suggest will be contacted for information only."

Absolutely always ask this question after each job research interview. If you feel uncomfortable, practice this question over and over, until it automatically flows from your lips at the end of the interview.

After the referral is given, ask permission to use his or her name when you make contact with that person.

You: "Thank you. I very much appreciate this additional help. And may I use your name when contacting Mr. Upton? I won't unless you give me permission. Would that be all right?"

Note: When getting the name and title of any referral, be sure to repeat the correct spelling.

Do not ask for a job from this contact. You said you only wanted information and you must keep your word. Now, however, is the time to ask the final "inside track" question . . . the job referral!

You: "Mr. Smith, as you can see, I'm determined to become a legal secretary. Can you think of anyone who might be interested in employing me?"

If a contact is given, again, get the correct spelling of the person's name, title, and company.

You: "May I use your name when I make my contact with .."

Strike while the iron's hot and get as much background as you can about your new referral:

1) Could you tell me a little about Mr/Mrs.?
2) Is he/she a business associate, a friend?
3) What products or services does the company provide. Any major new contracts? Expansions? Takeovers?

The answers to these questions are an important tool for getting on the inside track!

You have acquired a priceless wealth of information during this interview. Be sure and thank your contact.

"Thank you for taking the time to help me and for the referrals. May I keep you informed of the results of the contacts you suggested?"

The successful applicant knows that when a contact is kept advised about your job search, that person will take an active interest in helping you achieve your goal. Additional contacts usually follow.

If he or she agrees, do it! Always keep the contact advised of the results of leads you were given.

You: "Mr. Smith, I wanted to tell you I contacted Mr. Abels of XYZ company. Thank you for letting me use your name, it certainly helped me get the interview quickly. I also contacted Mr. Bean of Ester Company. Although his company isn't hiring now, he was quite pleased with my presentation and I feel confident he'll contact me at a later date. He said to tell you 'Hi'."

A positive attitude encourages further assistance.

Thank you notes and don't ever forget them.

The thank-you note is one of the most important - and neglected - parts of a job search. Not only is it common courtesy to thank someone who's taken the trouble to meet with you, but the note reminds the person of you and the purpose of your visit. So...

Within two days after the interview, always put a neatly typed thank-you note in the mail. Include some of the valuable information you gained, how you intend to utilize it, your gratitude for any referrals and a personal thank-you for the time spent with you.

Even if the interview did not go as well as you expected, send a thank you note anyway. You may feel the interview was unsuccessful but the interviewee may not.

Here's a sample letter:

Timothy Wells
00000 Franklin St.
Norfolk, PA 66243
802-681-4233

(date)

Mr. Harry Brown, Owner
Brown's Office Supply
44 Harold St.
Norfolk, VA 13982

Dear Mr. Brown:

Thank you for taking the time to see me yesterday. Since I plan to become a sales clerk in office supplies, your input will be of great help in achieving my objective.

Because of what you told me, I added two essential standards to my list of criteria for a sales person: anticipating the needs of customers; and keeping informed of new products.

Thank you again for your time.

Sincerely,

*What if I'm suddenly a candidate for a job at a
job research interview?*

It rarely happens but be prepared...just in case.

Contact: "Mr. Rice in marketing might have an opening and I
think he'd like to meet you. Are you interested?"

Once you recover and tell your contact you certainly are
interested, he or she may suggest you meet with this person
immediately. If at all possible, try to avoid this.

You: "I certainly do want to meet with Mr. Rice. Could we set
up an appointment for tomorrow or the next day? That will
give me time to put the information you just gave me in order
and pick up a copy of my resume."

Being prepared for an interview is essential. Ideally, you
should allow time to prepare a resume that utilizes the information you've gathered and a cover letter that reflects your research on the company. You have impressed your contact and
now you need to prepare yourself so you can go on to impress
the next interviewer. But it doesn't always work out that way.

If your contact insists on your seeing the potential job pros-
pect immediately (perhaps he or she is going out of town and
needs to fill the position immediately), you might have to go
ahead with the interview. Use the notes you just obtained as
much as you can, however.

CHAPTER 5

THE INSIDE TRACK -
WHAT TO DO WITH JOB REFERRALS

Making contact.

There are two ways to make contact with referrals. One is by telephone and the other by letter. Choose whichever makes you feel the most comfortable although a phone call usually gets quicker results. Letters allow the recipient to take his or her time responding, and in some instances, forget. However you choose to do it, when making contact with the referral, always mention the person who referred you (if permission was given), the purpose of your call or letter, the job criteria you learned and a request for an appointment. Let's begin with a phone call:

You: Good morning. May I speak with Ms. Mary James?
Operator: May I say who's calling?
You: Yes. Ruth Market.
Operator: May I tell her what this in regard to?
You: Certainly. Dr. John Abel of Hunt Dentistry referred me to Ms. James. He thought my interest in dentistry might be of value to your clinic.
Operator: One moment please.
James: This is Mary James. I understand Dr. Abel suggested you call me?
You: Yes. I recently spoke to Dr. Abel. He knows I'm interested in becoming a dentist's assistant, that I learn quickly, work well under pressure and have

flexible working hours. He suggested that your organization might be able to use someone like me. Could we make an appointment for . . .

Notice that Ruth used her inside track information - the job criteria - to get the listener's attention.

If you weren't given permission to use the referring person's name, your telephone contact would be slightly different.

You: Good morning. May I speak with Ms. Mary James?

Operator: May I tell her who's calling?

You: Yes. Ruth Market.

Operator: May I ask what this in regard to?

You: Yes. I have a background in dentistry that I believe would be helpful to her and your organization. Is she available?

Operator: We have no openings at this time. Send us your resume.

You: I'm aware there are no openings but I have some questions I'd like to ask her. May I speak with her for just a few minutes?

Operator: One moment please.

James: This is Mary James.

You: Thank you for taking my call Ms. James. I understand your organization is often in need of employees who can work under pressure, have flexible working hours and a background in dentistry. Since I meet all those standards, I hoped you would be willing to meet with me to discuss the possibility of my joining your staff? Could we meet on . . .

In both instances, Mary has used examples of her ability to perform the criteria of her profession. Ms. Market probably receives dozens of calls from applicants who asked for an interview and were turned down because the conversation did not generate interest in the candidate. Mary was not turned down.

But realistically, she could have been. No matter what she said or what reference she gave, even the most skillful job application will receive a "no thank you" from time to time. And that's okay. You may be calling someone who's late for an appointment or is simply cranky that day. Don't let it bother you, and never take it personally, they don't know you! Politely say something like 'it sounds like I called at a bad time. With your permission, I'll give you a call some other time. Thank you.'

For those of you who prefer to write letters to your referral, two sample letters follow, one when permission was given to name the referring person , the other when no name can be used. The letters do not change drastically, the real difference is in the eyes of the person receiving it. A referral letter simply has more clout. But this does not negate the importance of the well-written letter without a referral.

Letter with Referral Name

(date)

Ms. Mary Adams, Personnel Director
Acme Medical Center
29 Berkley St.
Jamesport, NY 00054

Dear Ms. Adams:

Dr. Abel suggested I get in touch with you. He felt my abilities as a clerical assistant could be of great value to your organization. He realizes a busy company like yours needs a clerical assistant who learns quickly, has flexible working hours and the ability to work well under pressure. I have those qualities.

My research into your company shows you have been in business well over fifteen years and have a strong professional relationship with your patients. The healing environment of your organization appeals to me, as I have long volunteered at a local hospital and enjoy helping others..

I am confident my desire to work hard, 'do it right' the first time, and willingness to learn, will be of great value to your organization. Could we meet some time next week so I can tell you a little more about myself and give you my resume? I realize your schedule is hectic and, if I have not heard from you by Friday, I will call and check in with you.

Thank you for taking the time to read this letter.

Sincerely,

May James

Letter Without Referral Name

(date)

Ms. Mary Adams, Personnel Director
Acme Medical Center
29 Berkley St.
Jamesport, NY 00054

Dear Ms. Adams:

I believe my abilities as a clerical assistant could be of great value to your organization. A busy company like yours needs a clerical assistant who learns quickly, has flexible working hours and the ability to work well under pressure. I have those qualities.

My research into your company shows you have been in business well over fifteen years and have a strong professional relationship with your patients. The healing environment of your organization appeals to me, as I have long volunteered at a local hospital and enjoy helping others.

I am confident my desire to work hard, do it right the first time, and eagerness to learn, will be of great value to your organization. Could we meet some time next week so I can tell you a little more about myself and give you my resume? I realize your schedule is hectic and, if I have not heard from you by Friday, I will call and check in with you.

Thank you for taking the time to read this letter.

Sincerely,

May James

CHAPTER 6

RESUMES: HOW TO MAKE
THEM SELL YOU!

Think of your resume as an advertising poster that's pinned to your back. You're walking around a hall with a lot of potential employers. That's good. But there are many other applicants in that hall also displaying an ad. That's not so good. The potential employers are going to base their hiring choice only on each applicant's 'ad' and no one is allowed to talk.

Get the picture? Your resume is your way of selling yourself. It tells others of your career goals, accomplishments, experiences, skills and education. You have so much to advertise and so little space to convey your messages. *Successful applicants know what information to advertise.* Here are tips to help you design your resume:

- **Always type your resume.** Hand-written resumes are not acceptable. Use a professional resume service if you can't type it yourself, but <u>use these guidelines.</u>
- **Keep it simple.** Fancy type and graphics tend to distract from the contents of your resume. Put your name, address and telephone number at the top of your resume. Be sure to include the area code with your telephone number.
- **Eliminate dates that give away your age**, such as when you graduated from schools. By not revealing your age, you keep the attention on how well your resume meets the job criteria instead of whether you meet somebody's preconceived notion of the ideal candidate.

- **Begin with your latest experience and work backwards.** Stop! My esp is rapping it's knuckles against my head. You're thinking 'I don't have any real job experience' or `I've been away from the work force for many years!' Doesn't matter. Remember what you have accomplished! Be creative and use your accomplishments instead of work dates! Or use both. **You have much to offer and don't you forget it!**
- **Use words from your Word Bank** whenever possible. They will add "sizzle" to your resume. **Include your accomplishments** along with your work history or experience. If you don't have the latter, just list your accomplishments. Come on, you worked hard to discover and define them, now use them!
- **Use the criteria list you developed.** When referring to your strengths and job qualifications, use the criteria for that job and, again, "sizzle" words from the word bank.
- **Omit salary requirements** and starting and ending salaries of previous employers.
- **Do not explain why you left each company.** You will however, want to be prepared for this question at your interview.
- **Be general** if you put an **"OBJECTIVE"** in your resume. You don't want to exclude yourself as a candidate for other positions in the company that might be of interest to you.
- **Don't list references.** "References upon request" is sufficient, but be prepared to give them at any time.

You can write your resume in several different ways. The two examples given below have proved effective for people with no or limited job experience and those who have been out of the job market for a while. As long as you include the tips listed above, your resume is sure to make the impression you want, get good results and stand out from the others.

50

Nancy Smith
1010 Wilson Avenue
Phoenix, AZ 40111
(515) 555-5555

Statement of Qualification
Self-starter, highly motivated, dedicated and hardworking. Listens to assignments and instructions carefully and prides herself on a job well done.

Experience
Mary Marshall, Phoenix, AZ - 1992 - Present
Child Care Supervisor

Supervised children, prepared meals, maintained the order of the household and scheduled activity events. Accomplishment: I developed a technique that actually made the children enjoy chores, including putting their toys away after each play period.

Education
Burkes High School, Phoenix, AZ
Majored in Business administration

Perfect Attendance Award

Skills
- Design and sew my own clothes.
- Can make a delicious meal out of anything.
- Ability to get along well with others

Joan Williams

4000 ABC Street, Grand Rapids, MI 48111, (808) 555-5555

Objective
> To secure a position with a progressive company where my communications and organizational skills can be utilized to their fullest.

Strengths
> •Well-developed written communication skills, including preparing job descriptions, speeches and training manuals.
> •Strong verbal communication skills, including extensive experience as class tutor.
> •Proficiency with computers (Own an IBM compatible, WordPerfect for Windows).

Experience
> Mrs. Joan Williams, Housewife & Mother 8/90 - to present
>
> Prepared nutritious and well balanced meals, balanced "taxi" efforts to minimize lost time, administered medication and practiced diplomacy between rivaling siblings.
>
> Accomplishments: I created a healthful, peaceful home environment, researched nutritional programs to assure well-balanced meals, and kept abreast of the latest information pertaining to education and family well-being.
>
> *Sales Clerk, Ames Boutique, Grand Rapids, Mi.*
>
> Interacted with customers, maintained inventory control, suggested new items that caused sales volume to grow and created window displays that won praise from customers and management.

Education
> University of Credits, Grand Rapids, MI
> Bachelor of Science

Now that I have my resume, do I still need to fill out employment applications?

Unfortunately, yes, most companies insist on it. An application identifies potential applicants for present and future openings. Your resume is the ad that accompanies the application and make it a "must read". When filling out an application, take time to answer each question fully. Don't leave any blanks. If a question does not apply to you, such as military background, fill in "not applicable" or N/A. Never write "See attached resume" in answer to any questions. This response indicates that you are lazy or don't feel the application is important.

Print your answers neatly, preferably in pen, so take a pen with you. Refer to your resume or have the dates of your work history and scholastic degrees on a card or sheet of paper for accuracy. If references are asked for (and they usually are) choose those where your desirable work habits, goals and career objectives can be verified whenever possible. You will probably need to include how long you've known your references, their occupations, addresses and telephone numbers.

CHAPTER SEVEN

COVER LETTERS THAT STAND OUT
FROM THE CROWD

Think of your cover letter as a building with six floors. In order to get to the top, you must first climb all six flights of stairs. *Successful applicants work their way up and finish at the top of the stack of resumes.*

FIRST FLOOR - ADDRESS YOUR LETTER TO A PERSON

This is another area where your research and contacts are of real value. Just as you are not impressed with mail addressed to "Occupant", the cover letter addressed "To whom it may concern" doesn't cut it either. So always direct your envelope and cover letter to an individual, making sure the name, title, company name and address are correct. If you're in doubt, call the office and ask.

Always use "Mr" or "Ms." in the address and the salutation (Dear Ms.....). Don't use first names unless you're writing your best friend or mother in which case you'd probably already have the job.

Since I worked most of my long career in human resources, I can tell you that mail directed to a specific person is usually put on top of the stack of mail and considered priority. When opened, resumes containing a cover letter are placed on top. The reason? Resumes with a cover letter save valuable time for the reader. They're like a marquee, presenting a brief preview of what's inside.

Referrals are important because they usually indicate that someone thinks of you as a valuable potential employee and this will give your resume priority over other applicants. The recipient of your cover letter and resume will usually recognize the name but it's still a good idea to include the company from which the referral originated.

Thank of a referral as frosting on a cake. If you frost, the cake will probably be eaten faster. But, if you don't, and it's a good cake, it will be devoured anyway.

SECOND FLOOR - RESEARCH INFORMATION

Select some of the research you've done on the company you're contacting and include it in your letter. Keep it brief and to the point, you're not trying to tell the reader something they already know but show you're interested enough in the company to have done research on it.

THIRD FLOOR - IDENTIFY THE POSITION YOU'RE SEEKING

Never assume that the person to whom you directed your letter knows which opening is of interest to you. Often a company has more than one opening and, if you don't clarify, your letter and resume may be pushed aside and possibly forgotten.

FOURTH FLOOR - MENTION YOUR ACCOMPLISHMENTS

Select appropriate accomplishments from the list you created earlier, choosing those which meet this particular job's hiring standards or criteria.

FIFTH FLOOR - MENTION YOUR STRENGTHS

Are you an organizer? Are you creative? Use your "what's important to you" accomplishments and the job criteria list to sell yourself in ways that will match what the company is seeking in an applicant.

SIXTH FLOOR - ASK FOR AN APPOINTMENT

A potential employer may receive a multitude of letters for a single job opening. Applicants who ask for an appointment in their letter indicate a strong desire to get the job. In the closing paragraph, say you're anxious to meet with this person and will call to schedule an appointment. If the opening is in another city or state, explain that you plan to be in that area during a certain week and will call in a few days to set up an appointment. **Keep a record of when you said you'd call that firm and then do it!**

TIPS:

1. Keep it short. The reader will probably have limited time to read your cover letter so confine it to one page.

2. Always type it. It takes time to decipher handwriting and most potential employers are busy, so type the letter or have it typed by the same service that does your resumes.

3. Use good quality paper and a matching envelope. The paper color should be white, light beige, bone or gray, and be of 25% cotton content. If you're choosey about the quality of paper you use, that means you're probably meticulous in your job performance too.

4. Before sealing that envelope, double check to make sure you signed it! If you forgot to sign your name, what important detail would you forget at work?

Sample letter

Mary Johnson
100 Melon Road
Elkhorn, IN 88888
(515) 555-555

(date)

Ms. Nancy Mitchell, Personnel Director
Ace Hi Markets
2222 Hill Road
Elkhorn, IN 88888

Dear Ms. Mitchell:

Mr. Pete Sims of Indiana Grocers suggested I contact you. He believes I could be of service to you as I am interested in becoming a sales clerk in the retail food industry. I grow all my own vegetables and am quite knowledgeable about nutrition.

I know your company began its chain of stores in Elkhorn in 1980 and now extends into four other states. A fast-growing organization sounds challenging and I like hard work and challenge!

In my recent job as a child-care overseer, I maintained order over three children. I was soon given the additional responsibility of scheduling activities that would help develop their motor skills. I am very proud of the fact that I developed a technique that encouraged the children to put their toys away properly...and like doing it!

Ms. Mitchell, I have tentatively set aside the week of June 24 for a possible meeting with you. Could we schedule an appointment sometime during that week? A call from you would be appreciated. If I have not heard from you within a few days, I will call you.

I'm enclosing my resume and look forward to meeting you and answering any questions you might have regarding it.

Sincerely,

Mary Johnson

I'm taking my resume to the interview - do I need my cover letter too?

Yes. A cover letter is a condensed version of your resume. It quickly shows the reader what you can do. By including a cover letter, you're telling the interviewer you know their time is valuable. That makes points for you.

The successful applicant develops a cover letter which permits the potential employer to begin the interview with little or no delay.

I sent my resume and cover letter to the interviewer earlier. Should I take another one?

Definitely. Never go to an interview thinking the interviewer has your resume handy. Resumes have a tendency to grow legs and "just walk away." It is embarrassing for the interviewer to announce its disappearance and poor organizational skills to admit you didn't bring a copy.

I found some classified ads that interest me. How do I structure my letter since no contact names are given?

Unfortunately, most classified ads don't give you a clue about where to direct your resume. If it only gives a post office box number and you want to send your resume, do so. Your letter and resume will still be light years better than your competition, even though they can't be directed to a specific person. If, by sheer luck, a company name has been included, treat the ad as you would one of your targeted companies and follow the procedures already outlined.

CHAPTER 8

PREPARING FOR AN INTERVIEW

All your preparations, research, networking and phone calls have paid off...you have a job interview!

Congratulations, you now have the opportunity to GET THAT JOB!...or blow it away. I don't want to scare you, but *the interview is the major deciding factor in determining who will be hired. So prepare prepare prepare!*

My years of interviewing showed me - clear as a bell - that if people spent as much time preparing for the interview as preparing their resume, "you're hired" would be a more common phrase. I often "pre-decided" which candidate I'd like to hire, based on their resume, only to find, during the interview, they knew nothing about the company or the job for which they were applying.

The most common mistake applicants make is coming to an interview unprepared.

Isn't it reassuring to know you have a better chance to GET THAT JOB when you've prepared for your interview? Let's talk about what will be expected of you.

"Applicants should know something about our company."

You're covered. If you did your homework about your targeted companies, you're prepared to give some details about the company from your earlier research.

"Accomplishments need to be brought forth."

Remember rehearsing your accomplishments a few chapters back? Now's the time to use it. Because you did this, you are well-prepared to volunteer your many accomplishments with ease.

"Many don't know what standards we're looking for in a candidate."

You do! And with that knowledge comes the ability to match your accomplishments to the job criteria.

"The applicant should also ask questions."

Many applicants are afraid to ask questions because they don't know what to ask. But questions from an applicant indicate an interest in the company and give you a chance to talk about how well you meet the job standards. You'll find some helpful questions at the end of Chapter 10. And there's another very good reason to ask questions about the job and the company: to find out whether or not you want this particular position. **Remember, your objective is to find the right job not just any job.** So, very very politely, try to determine whether this is that right job for you.

"They need to have confidence in their skills and abilities"

Interviewers expect a potential candidate to be a little nervous, yet not so timid that it takes a bulldozer to get them to talk about their accomplishments. Being prepared means having facts - about the company **and yourself** - at your fingertips. You'll be more at ease because you practiced, practiced and practiced.

61

"Applicants need to know the purpose of the interview."

You are at the interview to find out whether you want the job and, if you do, to get it. Focus on this and the fact that the interviewer is there to discover why he or she should hire you. That's all there is to it.

"Candidates are expected to be positive about themselves."

Interviewers do not want to hear what you cannot do but what you can do. "I can't do that" is not a good answer but "With some help from your staff, yes, I can do that." is.

"When asked about their salary requirements, most applicants have no idea about their salary range."

Your job research interviews gave you this information. Knowing the range means your requirements will be neither too low or high.

Now that you know what the interviewer expects of you, what should you expect of yourself when preparing for your interview?

Successful applicants:

Review their research. Select data you feel comfortable discussing. The more at ease you are, the more confidence you exude. Company background and knowledge of the product or service offered are key areas of research to target.

Rehearse accomplishments. From your list of accomplishments, copy those which most closely match the company's criteria, then rehearse, rehearse and rehearse.

Prepare a list of questions to ask about the company. For example, who are their competitors, what new advances are being made, and what are the most common challenges of the department where you hope to work.

Anticipate possible negative areas about their background. The successful applicant addresses any areas which may be of concern to the interviewer and rehearses possible responses. Example: "You have had very little experience, I see."

This could be a statement or a question. Do not, and I repeat, do not become defensive. Your reaction to this question gives the interviewer the answer, regardless of what you say! Looking upset or glaring could make the potential employer think you might be too immature to consider hiring.

Don't apologize for whatever is questioned, e.g. your inexperience or long time out of the job market, give a **positive** answer such as:.

"I have been working very hard to develop excellent skills and, because I am new to the job market, I bring a lot of enthusiasm and ideas. From the research I've done, I think I have a lot to offer (company name)

Know how to lead an interview to her/his advantage. Wouldn't it be wonderful if every interviewer gave you the chance to show off your accomplishments while you, in turn, learned more about the company? But the truth is that quite a few interviewers don't know much about how to interview. When this happens, it will be up to you to gently lead and direct the interview. Notice the words "gently lead and direct." Here are a few tips.

The interviewer seems nervous, unsure of what to ask.

Eye contact is important. If the interviewer seems nervous, begin volunteering some information about the company e.g. "I think your new software "Easy Does It Computing" sounds wonderful. I sure could have used it when I bought my computer and had to learn all the basics on my own!"

Notice how the applicant slipped in the accomplishment?

The interviewer is telling me all about the company, but not what I want to know about.

Listen carefully to the information being given, then find an opening that allows you to ask a question such as:

"I can see why you think the company's sales goals for next year are pretty ambitious but then you are one of the leaders in the field. How many consumers are currently using your new software?"

Remember to ask questions from which you gain insights into the company's success, failures, goals, etc. After all, you have a decision to make about whether or not, if offered, you want to accept a job here.

Prepare to ask for a job. (See Chapter 11 "How to ask for the job" but not until you finish this section, please)

Now you know all about the interviewer's and your own expectations. You have the tools and are prepared...almost. The following chapters will provide the rest of the tools you need to become the successful applicant.

CHAPTER 9

MAKING THE *RIGHT* FIRST IMPRESSION

You may be - far and away - the best candidate for the job. But if the first impression you make is unfavorable, you probably won't get a chance to demonstrate your superior skills and knowledge.

Let's explore the most common errors made by unsuccessful job applicants. Being in personnel myself, I've seen and heard all the complaints and concerns of other personnel managers and executives interviewing job applicants. We'll begin with the most obvious part of that all-important first impression:

YOUR APPEARANCE

Personal hygiene and your appearance go together, they're a team. You might know someone who dresses impeccably but has breath that could drop a hyena in its tracks.

• **Brush your teeth right before an interview.** Carry floss or a toothbrush with you if you eat out before going to the interview. Food stuck between your teeth is unattractive, distracting and embarrassing for you.

• **Use a breath freshener, gum or breath mint** before going to the interview...**NEVER DURING**

• **Clean your nails.** If you wear nail polish, make sure it's not chipped. Very long finger nails, unless you're applying for a job as a hand model, are not advisable during the interviewing process. I felt - and other interviewers agree - that we tend to be concerned about women with excessively long nails because they indicate someone not used to working.

• **Arrange your hair** neatly so it doesn't repeatedly fall over your face. Constantly brushing your hair away from your face is an annoying mannerism to many people...including interviewers.

• **Ladies: always carry spare pantyhose,** just in case.

• **No smoking allowed.** Even if you are told that you can...never smoke during an interview.

• **Use little or no scent.** Many people have negative reactions to certain fragrances and using too much scent is always offensive. (That's just as true of after-shave as perfume)

DRESSING THE PART

Dressing properly for an interview is not difficult if you keep these tips in mind:

Wear appropriate, stylish clothing. You don't have to be wealthy to look professional. Select outfits that make you feel good about yourself but aren't overly dressy or casual. They should be well fitted (never wear a skirt or dress that's too tight or short), simple styles that are attractive without being faddish and are appropriate for the kind of job you're seeking. Your shoes, of course, will be polished.

Avoid too much jewelry. Discreet jewelry makes a much better first impression than rings and bells on every finger or huge dangling earrings

Clean and press your outfit each time you wear it.

Use makeup moderately.

HOW YOU BEHAVE IS AS IMPORTANT AS HOW YOU LOOK

Part of the "first impression" you make is the message conveyed by your behavior. **Here are some things you should never never do:**

Arrive late for the interview: Punctuality is of utmost importance to your potential employer. Make a habit of arriving early for the scheduled appointment, it's far better for you to wait then your prospective boss.

Demonstrate lack of organization skills: Interviewers tell me it's frustrating to wait while an applicant searches through an attache case or handbag for pen or resume and they certainly don't want to hear "I left my resume in the car. I'll be right back." Organizational skills are a necessity in any career, so get yourself together before you arrive at the interview.

Interrupting the interviewer: Listen to what is being said until the person comes to a full stop. Vital information can be missed if an applicant keeps interrupting. Not only is it annoying, but your prospective employer will get the impression that, since you don't listen, how could you hear instructions on the job and follow them properly?

BODY LANGUAGE

Body language is the way we send out signals about ourselves to others. They can be more powerful than any spoken word. Interviewers often look at a candidate's body language and you may be surprised to learn that the wrong kind can be responsible for people not getting a job. Here are some common body language signals to avoid.

SLOUCHING

You're not even aware you're doing it, you just feel surprisingly relaxed, calm and quite comfortable. Not surprising since you're practically lying down.

The interviewer receives the signal that you really don't want this job. You appear bored, as if you were just going through the formalities until the interview is over.

CLOCK WATCHING

You have to pick up your son at the day care center. You keep looking at the clock on the wall because it's almost time and you're getting nervous. If the interview is finished in another twenty minutes, you can still make it to the school on time.

The interviewer gets the impression that he or she is boring you. Or perhaps you have a more pressing engagement with another firm and this job isn't good enough for you.

HANDS BEHIND THE HEAD

You find that putting your hands behind your the head relaxes you and helps you feel comfortable and speak more easily.

The interviewer is getting a signal that you are so much at ease that you obviously feel superior to him or her.

BITING YOUR NAILS

Biting your nails may be such a nervous habit, you don't realize you're doing it.

The interviewer is given the impression that you are an overly nervous person who might not be capable of working under pressure.

FIDDLING WITH AN OBJECT

When you put on that expensive tie pin, the catch felt wobbly. You keep checking to make sure you haven't lost it.

The signal being sent is that you are unsure of yourself. In this situation, a different tie pin would have been a wise decision.

ARMS FOLDED IN FRONT OF THE BODY

You are trying really hard not to use your hands to express yourself. Many have teased you about this habit and you don't want the interviewer to think you're undignified or overly emotional.

On the contrary. The interviewer believes that you are close-minded and that communication would be more productive with a goldfish. If you have a need to control your hands, place one on top of the other and keep both in your lap.

SWINGING OR TAPPING YOUR FOOT

You just crossed your legs and now you feel more relaxed except, unknowingly, you're swinging your foot back and forth. Or, you really want this job and are getting anxious about how to let the interviewer know that, and your foot is tapping in rhythm with your anxiety.

You are sending the signal that you are not too interested in what is being said and in a hurry to end the interview. If you have the habit of swinging your leg to relax yourself, simply avoid crossing your legs. Tapping your foot also signals impatience or that the applicant is unhappy with the interviewer and eager to end the conversation.

AVOIDING EYE CONTACT

You really wish that you weren't so shy. The interviewer keeps looking at you and that makes you even more nervous.

The interviewer thinks you might not be telling the truth, the whole truth and nothing but the truth. Eye contact at an interview is extremely important. A person who speaks directly and looks into the listener's eyes is exuding interest and confidence. Practice, practice and practice until you can look into the eyes of others when speaking.

If you think you might be guilty of any of the above at an interview, don't fret. Now that you are aware of your bad habits you can break them.

Handshaking is another form of body language. Four handshakes have been named by people who interview frequently which should give you a hint about how meaningful handshakes are. They are called the **Dead Mackerel, Bone Crusher,** the **Sandwich,** and the **Grabber.** The Dead Mackerel, the limp handshake, suggests a person with a weak personality. The Bone Crusher gives the impression of aggression. The Sandwich, in which both hands are used, is a very personal handshake and inappropriate for most business situations. The Grabber, where the arm is grabbed while shaking the hand, is overly intimate for a job interview with a stranger.

After an interview, wait for the interviewer to extend his or her hand first. Don't shake the hand up and down, just give it a discreet shake and squeeze enough to give a confident impression. Incredible as it seems, hiring decisions have been made based on the simple, everyday handshake.

CHAPTER 10

THE TWELVE QUESTIONS INTERVIEWERS ARE MOST LIKELY TO ASK YOU

It's unreasonable to think anyone could know all the questions that might be asked at an interview. But there are a number that are frequently asked. Knowing what they are will prepare you and help reduce your anxiety.

Here's one of the most commonly asked questions:

1. "TELL ME ABOUT YOURSELF"

Where do you start? Not at the beginning, please. Keep your answer positive and brief. Refer to your "what's important" and accomplishments lists and use them for your answer and don't worry, you can't forget them, they're all about you. Don't forget the job criteria. You don't want to say you like working alone if the job criteria requires someone to work with many other employees.

Possible answer: "I'm an energetic person who works well under pressure, I enjoy working with others as a team and I'm extremely well-organized."

2. "WHAT IS A QUALITY YOU NEED TO DEVELOP?"
(Or, what is your worst quality you need to work on?)

The interviewer is looking for a positive answer. Once again, use your "what's important" and accomplishments lists to select qualities and experiences that reflect good work habits. Do long hours and working weekends not bother you?

Possible answer: "I have to finish a job even if it means taking work home nights or weekends. My mother complains about this and I need to work out a strategy to get others to do my chores at home!" A sense of humor is almost always a tension reliever. In fact, getting a little chuckle during an interview can be an asset.

Now for the "What is the worst quality you need to work on?" part of the question. The same principle applies. Choose something "important to you" from your list that's positive. Do you like working in a small office with only a few employees? Use that, if it meets the job criteria.

Possible answer: "I enjoy working in a small office, it just seems more pleasant to me but I'm learning to concentrate when there are a lot of people around ."

3. WHAT'S YOUR IDEA OF THE IDEAL JOB?

Again, refer to your lists and use your knowledge about the company and the kind of job being offered. Choose something that's important to you and matches the criteria.

Possible answer: "A job that lets me travel and work in a fast-paced environment would be great for me."

4. WHY SHOULD I HIRE YOU?

What the interviewer is really asking is "What can you do for my company?" Answer by using your accomplishment and "what's important" list. Here's Mrs. Unknown's answer, remember her from Chapter One?

Possible answer: "I'm a creative person, I've always been good at interior decorating and I understand this position would require me to set up the display windows for the store. I know I could do an outstanding job, our little theatre group won an award for the stage set I designed last year."

Other attributes can be mentioned here: Are you a person who strives for perfect attendance? (If you have a certificate for achieving perfect attendance, bring it with you and show it to the interviewer.) Are you a person who always gets to work on time? Are you dedicated, have a high energy level and take pride in what you do? Personal attributes of your own are perfect for an answer.

Possible answer: "I'm a very hard worker who's always on time and, whatever I do, I strive for perfect attendance. I understand this position calls for these qualities."

5. WHAT DO YOU KNOW ABOUT OUR COMPANY?

We've said it again and again: researching a potential employer is vitally important. But, if you didn't do you homework properly, get to the interview earlier than usual and ask the receptionist about the company. She may just hand you some brochures but it's quicker to ask a few basic questions such as, how long in business, how many employees and what service or product does the company offer. In most cases, the receptionist will gladly answer your questions.

Possible answer: "I know this branch of the company has been here for two years, that your corporate office is in Seattle and that you offer a unique computer software. I'm very interested in learning more."

6. WHAT SALARY ARE YOU LOOKING FOR?

Give a range of salary requirement. You should have the salary ranges from the job research interviews you conducted.

Possible answer: "I've been interviewing others in this field and their salaries range from $1800 to $2400 per month."

By giving a range, you establish the least and most you expect, based on your experience and knowledge at the present time.

7. WHICH IS MORE IMPORTANT TO YOU IN A JOB... MONEY OR THE TYPE OF WORK?

Saying "both" to this question is a good response. Money should not be the only reason you accept a position but to pretend that money doesn't matter is insincere and won't fool anyone.

Possible answer: "Both. I want to be challenged and enjoy my work, but I also want to be compensated fairly.".

8. WOULD YOU CONSIDER LESS MONEY?

When an interviewer asks you this, chances are he or she is interested in you, but perhaps your salary requirements are higher than expected. Now is the time for you to ask questions of the interviewer.

Possible answer: "Finding the right company is important to me. I plan to be there for a long time. What figure did you have in mind?"

Then ask how many promotions were made at this job level over the last year and when salary reviews are held. By asking these questions, you are letting the interviewer know you are interested in the position but expect to be compensated at a later date for your accomplishments and ability.

9. HOW DO YOU DEFINE SUCCESS?

Translation: the interviewer wants to know your goals in life. My personal definition of success is setting goals and achieving them. For some, it might be financial security or taking pride in their accomplishments.

Once I asked a potential employee this question and her reply was, "My definition of success is looking forward to going to work!" I thought that was a good one. So don't base your definition of success on tangible items. Other examples of success could be doing what makes you happy or feel good about yourself.

10. WHAT DID YOU LIKE THE MOST/LEAST ABOUT YOUR LAST JOB?

Your list of "what's important" will again help you answer both of these questions.

Possible answer: "Parenting and homemaking are surprisingly complex jobs, you have to juggle a lot of balls in the air to do them right. I liked that. I am someone who enjoys a challenge and looks for additional responsibilities."

When addressing what you least liked about your last job, use something important to you that you did not enjoy at your last job.

Possible answer: "I like the stimulation of working with other people and there was little contact with anyone at ABC Company."

11. WHAT HAVE YOU DONE THAT SHOWS INITIATIVE?

Every day you do something that shows initiative. Take the housewife who wants her family to have a well-balanced diet, she takes the *initiative* to read literature on nutrition and apply the principles she learns. A cheerleader wants to create new cheers. She took the *initiative* to visit other teams to get fresh ideas. A business had new computers installed and someone took the *initiative* to read the manual, practice and help others learn. In answer to this question, describe what you did to achieve your own accomplishments. If possible, gear your answer to the job requirements.

Possible answer: "Just about every business uses computers now so, before I started my job search, I purchased one and, in my spare time, read the tutorials and became computer literate."

12. DO YOU HAVE ANY QUESTIONS?

This is the time to get some insights into the position. **Don't ask about benefits at this point**. Interviewers might interpret that as your being more interested in benefits than the job or company. Instead, ask questions about the company such as: are there any new products or services being developed; who is their biggest competitor, etc. Inquiries about the job itself are also possible questions.

• Is this a new position?
• Am I replacing someone?
• What would you say is the least and most attractive part of this job?

It's usually best to include a mixture of questions, some about the company and some regarding the position.

After you ask any of these questions, *listen very carefully to the answers.*

Now that you know the questions that will probably be asked and those you might ask, here's one last bit of advice. *Be yourself* during an interview. Memorizing sample answers could cost you the interview if you fail to remember one. But, even if you do remember, the interviewer will probably know your reply is not spontaneous. Answer the questions in your own words using **rehearsed** accomplishments.

CHAPTER 11

NOW ASK FOR THE JOB!

Asking for the job is probably the most important part of an interview, yet many are afraid to do it. The successful applicant asks for the job! Not by saying "can I work here?" of course, but by making it clear to the interviewer that you are definitely interested and want to become part of the organization.

Keep the purpose of the interview in mind. Yes, you did want to find out all you could about the position (which you are now sure you want) and you did want to make a good impression, but what are you are really after? An offer! You want the interviewer to ask you to come to work.

In many cases that won't happen. Often, the interviewer has to confer with an associate before making a decision **so don't be disappointed or frustrated if you don't get a job offer by the end of the interview.** If you have not been offered the job, then ask for it with the following questions. The best time is after you have shaken hands (no Mackerals please) and you are about to leave. Rehearse these questions until they just flow from your lips. The most effective practice plan is to ask friends to help. Shake their hands, turn as if leaving, and then turn back and ask the questions. Do this so often you'll associate the handshake with the questions.

1. Excuse me, but are many other people interviewing for this position?
2. When do you feel a final decision will be made?
3. Will I be considered for the job?
4. Will I be informed of that decision, even if I am not chosen?

After each question, *listen* to the answer and *look* directly into the eyes of the interviewer. Then thank the interviewer and leave.

When you get home, pat yourself on the back! You just made it through what might be considered the toughest part of your job campaign. Take a few minutes to put your thoughts in order and then complete the last part of the interview...the thank-you note:

- Thank the interviewer for seeing you:

"Thank you for the opportunity of meeting with you and discussing my qualifications."

- Remind the interviewer of your accomplishments:

"As a caretaker, I kept myself up to date on current rehabilitation techniques, and incorporated as much as possible in my patient's daily routine."

- Put your accomplishment and the interviewer's criteria together:

"Because I am a person with initiative, and because you require a self-starter, I believe I could be of value to your organization."

- Let the interview know you are interested:

"I would be very pleased to accept a job offer from your company, and eagerly wait to hear from you."

Remember, there are no exceptions with thank you notes. **Do it!**

CHAPTER 12
THE SECOND INTERVIEW,
WHAT DO I DO NOW?

First of all, congratulate yourself again. The second interview means the prospective employer was impressed with you. You now have your foot in the door and beyond. But before you get too confident, beware. Don't make the mistake of thinking that because the first interviewer may have thought you were the best person for the job, the second interviewer will automatically come to the same conclusion. Prepare properly, however, and you have every reason to believe they will.

SECRET: The successful applicant prepares for the second interview as if it were the first.

Here are some of the questions most applicants ask about the second interview:

CAN I WEAR THE SAME OUTFIT AS I DID TO THE FIRST?

The second interview is almost always with another person but often the first interviewer introduce the applicant to the second. If you must wear the same outfit, try to change the blouse or shirt and accessories to give a different appearance.

WHAT DO I SAY?

Again, be yourself. The answers you rehearsed about what's important to you and what you've accomplished have not changed. In some instances, the first interviewer may be present during the second. This should not change how you respond to questions. Remember, your first interview made a positive impression, so why change now? If the interviewer does remember some of the conversation, it will only remind her or him of how proud you are of your accomplishments. That is probably why you made a good impression in the first place.

DO I ASK FOR THE JOB AGAIN?

Absolutely! You are after a job offer and the way to get that offer is to ask for it. It's okay to ask for the job in the same manner as the first interview.

1. Are there many others interviewing for this position?
2. When do you feel a final decision will be made?
3. Will I be considered for the job?
4. Will I be informed of that decision, even if I am not chosen?

DO I NEED TO SEND A THANK-YOU NOTE, AGAIN!

You bet you do. The thank-you note you sent to the first interviewer was to thank *that* interviewer. Now, send a thank-you note to *this* one.

You know the old saying "there's an exception to every rule." Not with thank-you notes there aren't. After each and every interview, get one in the mail within two days. If your second interview is with the same person as before, you must send a thank-you note again. No exceptions.

WHAT HAPPENS IF I DON'T GET THE JOB?

It happens. Don't blame yourself. You did a good job preparing for the interview, you heard positive responses, and you were considered for the job. Many applicants don't get that far.

If you've been informed that you were not selected before you send in your thank you note, send the thank-you anyway. Why do this if you didn't get the job? Because most interviewers will keep your letter, just in case the first choice doesn't work out or another similar position turns up.!

> **SECRET: Successful applicants believe they were the second choice.**

Robert Williams
1420 John Road
Detroit, WI 72981
(683) 622-8466

(date)

Mr. Michael Jones
Wonderful World Toys
111 Anywhere St.
Toys, MI 42183

Dear Mr. Jones:

I was very disappointed to hear I will not be working for your company. Although I was not chosen to become a part of Wonderful World Toys team at this time, I hope I will be considered as a candidate for any future openings.

Thank you, Mr. Jones for your time and effort. It is very much appreciated.

Sincerely,

Robert Williams

CHAPTER 13
YOU GOT THE JOB! CONGRATULATIONS!
NOW KEEP UP THE GOOD WORK!

You did it! You are now one of those *successful applicants* we've been talking about throughout the book. But there's one thing more. Now that you have a job, how do you keep it? There are no guarantees in life, especially when it comes to one's career, but there are some principles and standards that can help.

Don't lose sight of what is important to you. Remember, your standards are what got you hired for in the first place. Treat each work day as a new challenge, reinforcing your old values and building new ones. Let your actions reflect your energy and integrity.

how to GET THAT JOB? That's just the beginning of your success story.

Pilot Books Reading Shelf
To order, simply call our toll-free number
(800) 79PILOT

the bare bones guide to Better Business Writing by Sally Williams. The book you'll refer to again and again when writing for business (or on personal matters). Answers the questions we all have about proper grammar, punctuation, vocabulary. Fast, no-fluff format gives quick ways to improve your writing skills. ISBN: 0-87576-203-4. $7.95

Help Wanted/ Korea by Sam Hawley. If you're a college graduate with a taste for adventure, there are thousands of well-paying jobs in exotic South Korea. A fascinating comprehensive guide. ISBN: 0-87576-208-5. $9.95

Guide to Cruise Ship Jobs. Author George Reilly, a Chief Purser, provides inside information on planning your job search, what positions are available, necessary qualifications and how to make your experience and education fit them. Includes a listing of major cruise lines and recruiting firms for cruise ship companies. ISBN: 0-87576-188-7. $7.95

How to Get the Job You Want Overseas. There are overseas jobs in private industry and the federal government. This step-by-step guide describes where the jobs are, who is offering them, salary scales and employment benefits. ISBN: 087576-148-8. $4.95

Starting and Operating A Clipping Service. This manual shows you exactly how to establish your own clipping service. What to look for in your daily and weekly newspapers and detailed instructions on how and where to submit clippings. ISBN: 0-87576-133-X. $3.95

Starting and Operating a Playgroup for Profit. Make kids your business. Full or part-time, playgroups are enjoyable ways to earn money, take little investment and are greatly needed in most communities. This guide shows how. ISBN: 0-87576-055-4. $3.95

Starting and Operating A Vintage Clothing Shop. If vintage clothing fascinates you...here's a book that tells exactly how to start and run a vintage clothing shop, full or part-time. ISBN: 0-87576-104-6. $3.50